I0435931

THE CRYPTOZOOLOGY WORLD

CRYPTIDS STARTING WITH "A"

VOLUME 1

MITCHELL WAITE

ISBN-10: 1493637312

ISBN-13: 978-1493637317

DEDICATION

I WOULD LIKE TO DEDICATE THIS BOOK TO
A VERY GOOD FRIEND OF MINE WHO WAS
RESPONSIBLE FOR MY INTRODUCTION INTO
THE WORLD OF CRYPTOZOOLOGY. THANK
YOU SUSAN FARNSWORTH.

CONTENTS

INTRODUCTION

This book contains my research notes and articles used in my studies of cryptids and Cryptozoology. This volume will cover all cryptids in my files starting with an "A", and will be in alphabetic order.

CRYPTOZOOLOGY Introduction

Cryptozoology is not a recognized branch of science or zoology, but is considered to be a pseudoscience. However, the study is a necessity for those animals whose existence has not yet been proven, animals that are considered extinct, or those who are mentioned in myths and legends but do not have any scientifically recognized evidence of existence. Cryptozoology will also encompass the study of misplaced animals, or those animals that are appearing where they should not be.

The term used for each animal species in the Cryptozoology studies is cryptid. A cryptid (from the Greek meaning "hide") is a creature or plant whose existence has been reported, but is unrecognized by mainstream science and often regarded as highly unlikely to exist.

Some examples of animals that have not yet been proven are the Mogollon Monster, Bigfoot, Yeti, Yowie, Grass Man, Loc Ness Monster, Ogopogo, Skin Fin, and the Chupacabra.

Examples of those that were considered extinct, but are rumored to exist are the Thunderbirds (possible pterodactyls), Mokèlé-mbèmbé (a possible brontosaurus), Ogopogo, Nessie, Champ, Skin Fin (possible plesiosaurs) and the coelacanth (prehistoric fish).

Mythological creature studies deals with folk lore, myths, and legends of supernatural creatures of both past and present. Some examples of the past are griffins, dragons, trolls, fairies, and unicorns. Present Mythological creatures are the Jersey Devil, the Moth Man, the Wendigo, Dog Faced Bigfoot, Vampires, and Werewolves.

Misplaced animals may be the jaguars in Arizona, alligators in New York City, javilina (a rodent looking like a small bore pig) in the Southwest United States, and pythons in Florida. Some other interesting animals are the ivory-billed woodpecker, and the giant vampire bat.

There have been several cryptids which have been removed from the Cryptozoology studies, and are now verified as to exist in the real science of zoology. Some examples of these animals are the okapi (discovered in 1901), mountain gorilla (October 1902), giant squid (2004), and the Hoan Kiem Turtle (1967). Please note these dates are when the Scientific Community declared them real, not when the locals reported their first sightings. In many cases, the locals knew of cryptids existence centuries before they were proven to exist by science.

THE ADJULE

The Adjule also known as the Kelb-el-khela (male) and the Tarhsit (female) are canine-like creatures which inhabit only desert regions, and they are almost exclusively reported to inhabit North Africa in the Sahara Desert. These first reports/sightings of the dog-like creatures were made by the local people known as the Tuaregs near Mauritania. These sightings were recorded by Théodore Monod in 1928. However, recent reports place them in Koro Toro, CHAD, and Death Valley, USA.

One unconfirmed sighting occurred in 1992. The report was from the resident hunters of the village in Western Mauritania. The animals were described as being dog-like creatures which hunt in packs. Unfortunately, this report was never confirmed for *Lycaon pictus* species (IUCN/CSG, 1997).

The cryptid is described as being approximately two and a half feet tall, with feet that are webbed, and having rough thick crimson colored skin which has a bluish tint. Descriptions have the wolf-like creature weighing in at about thirty to forty five pounds

The Adjule are not lone creatures. The hunting packs number from three to thirteen. The only natural enemy is reported to be the Hive Monster. The Hive Monster is an insect like creature that spawns larva which bore into the brains of humans and other creatures.

The Adjule sometimes (called the Bush Dog) is reported to have some supernatural powers. The local tribesmen of the Sahara say it uses pheromones to cause great contention or discord among the area's residents allowing them to hunt their prey. There are no records or mention of the Adjule attacking humans.

There are no known photos of the Adjule, and most of the scientific world will debunk the idea of such a creature existing saying it is more than likely a African Wild Dog of a known species which has mange, or the creature has been misidentified by the local population of humans. In many cases involving cryptids, the local people have known about the reclusive animals in the region as long as the locals can remember. Many have developed into mythical creatures of legend and lore. However, these legends are usually based on truth, but science will not accept the existence of the creatures until science discovers them. Who is correct? The choice boils down to the local human population who knows the area, animals, and lives off the land; or scientists/biologists whom have never been in the area except for an expedition or two. My bet would be on the locals.

INFORMATION SOURCES:

http://en.wikipedia.org/wiki/Adjule

http://www.nick.com/troop-grid/monsters/adjule.jhtml

http://mysticaluniverse.com/creatures/adjule/

Théodore Monod, "Sur la présence du Sahara du Lycaon pictus (Temm.) (Résultats scientifiques de la Mission Saharienne Augiéras-Draper)," Bulletin de la Société Zoologique de France 53 (1928): 262–264.

Woodroffe, R., Ginsberg, J.R. and Macdonald, D.W. (1997) The African wild dog: status survey and conservation action plan - IUCN Canid Specialist Group. IUCN, Gland, Switzerland.

Eberhart, George M., *Mysterious Creatures: A Guide to Cryptozoology*, 2 vols (ABC-Clio: Santa Barbara, 2002).

THE AGOGWE

This human-like biped is found in East Africa usually near or in dense jungle. Locals refer to them with different names including Agogure, Agogue, Kakundakari, Kilombia, and Sehite. There have been several reported sightings in 1900, 1938, and tracks found in the 1950 through 1960. Captain William Hichens reported his experience in the December 1937 edition of Discovery Magazine, and a confirming report was made by Cuthbert Burgoyne who wrote a letter to the magazine in 1938 recounting his sighting of something similar in 1927. Charles Cordier, a renouned animal collector reported to have tracked the biped in the late 1959s and early 1960s in Zimbabwe. One of his accounts states a Agogwe had become ensnared in a bird trap, but before they could get the creature. The creature had done a face plant in dirt, but it rolled over sat up and took the noose off its foot and fled. This seems to indicate some intelligence above typical animals.

The Agogwe is a small biped with a rounded forehead and small canines, and is reported to be human-like. It ranges from a about 3 feet to almost 6 feet in height, and has toes that are opposable on feet approximately 5 inches long. The cryptid has long arms typical of a primate. The hair ranges from black, grey, to rust-colored and is quite wooly. Under the hair is a yellowish-red skin.

The Agogwe may be the descendants of the Gracile Australopithecine which existed back 3.9 million years ago. However, the opposable big toe may be an indication they are different species. It is possible the Agogwe evolved the opposable big toe over time to aid in living and climbing trees.

Reports of small bipedal ape apes resembling the Agogwe have come from Sumatra. The locals call them the Orang Pendek. However, it is not known if the two species are one and the same. The Orang Pendek has been reported to have a hood of hair or mane.

The Agogwe has not been proven to exist. However, this could be attributed to the vast rain forests of East Africa. Other than the local natives, explorers, and hunters, the jungles of East Africa remain untraveled and could contain many unidentified species of cryptids.

INFORMATION SOURCES:

http://www.unknown-creatures.com/agogwe.html

http://en.wikipedia.org/wiki/Agogwe

Hichens, W (Dec 1937). "African Mystery Beasts.". *Discovery*: 369–373. Archived from the original on 25 January 2010. Retrieved 2010-01-25.

Bradley, M. (2003). *Esau's Empire*.

Cremo, M.; Thompson, R. (1996). *Forbidden Archaeology: The Hidden History of the Human Race*. Bhaktivedanta Book Publishing. Archived from the original on 5 February 2010. Retrieved 2010-01-25.

"Hairy Hominids". americanmonsters.com. Retrieved 2010-01-25.

"Agogwe". Archived from the original on 15 January 2010. Retrieved 2010-01-25.

Cameron McCormick. "African Ape Complex". Archived from the original on 2009-10-24.

THE AHOOL

The Ahool (Pterapus Boomus) is described as being
a type of Pterosaur, flying primate, or large bat type
creature. The body is covered with black or grey fur,
and it is about the size of a one year old human. The
creature has large claws are large at the end of its
forearms. The wings span from three to ten feet. In
some cases reports state the wings are leathery skin,
while others state the wings are covered with a type
of downy fluff. The Ahool is reported to have the
head of a monkey, and the face of a man with large
black eyes. The feet are said to be pointed
backwards.

Ahools are reported to be a matriarchal social order where the females and their young stay together until the youth is capable to breed. The Males live alone.

Even though the Ahool are successful predators, they are considered to be omnivores. However, they will eat large quantities of meat. The plants in their diet is not known, but their prey will include small animals such as cats all the way up the food chain to humans. Hunting techniques allegedly involve hanging upside down in the jungle canopy and dropping down on the selected prey sinking their teeth into the neck severing the arteries or snapping the neck. In this manner, they are not required soar the skies allowing them to stay nearly invisible to the prey.

In 1925 Dr. Ernest Bartels had to sightings near the Salak Mountains on the Island of Java, Indonesia. He reported a huge bat-like creature made a pass by his head while he was exploring some waterfalls. Two weeks later, the creature was seen again. The Doctor heard what sounded like "A-hoool". As he investigated the sound, the creature took off and flew away. This is where the creature got its name.

Even though Dr Bartels' encounter happened on the island of Java, the Ahool is reported to be found throughout most of dense jungles of Indonesia. New Guinea has the Ropen which many crypto zoologists consider to be a Sub-species of the Ahool. The Ropen has large wings, long snout, and displays a long thing crest of raised hair.

INFORMATION SOURCES:

http://en.wikipedia.org/wiki/Ahool

http://animal.discovery.com/tv-shows/other/videos/freak-encounters-ahool.htm

http://www.unknown-creatures.com/ahool.html

http://cryptidz.wikia.com/wiki/Ahool

COLEMAN, LOREN & CLARK, JEROME (1999): *Cryptozoology A to Z: the encyclopedia of loch monsters, Sasquatch, Chupacabaras, and other authentic mysteries of nature.* Fireside, New York. ISBN 0-684-85602-6

HOLT, DENVER W., BERKLEY, REGAN; DEPPE, CAROLINE; ENRÍQUEZ ROCHA, PAULA L.; OLSEN, PENNY D.; PETERSEN, JULIE L.; RANGEL SALAZAR, JOSÉ LUIS; SEGARS, KELLEY P. & WOOD, KRISTIN L. (1999):

Family Strigidae (typical owls). *In:* DEL HOYO, J.; ELLIOTT, A. & SARGATAL, J. (EDS): *Handbook of Birds of the World, Volume 5:*

Barn-owls to Hummingbirds: 76-242, plates 4-20. Lynx Edicions, Barcelona. ISBN 84-87334-25-3

SHUKER, KARL (2003): *The Beasts That Hide From Man.* Paraview, New York.ISBN 1-931044-64-3

THE AKKOROKAMUI

The Akkorokamui has not been confirmed and is thought to be either a giant squid or giant octopus living in the waters of Funka Bay near the Japanese island Hokkaido located on the north end of Japan. It has also been reported in the waters around Thailand.

It can be seen at long distances because of its size and color. The skin is said to be a incandescent red likened to the color of a red sunset. The cryptid's size has been reported to be approximately four hundred feet.

Although this all sounds much like the chapter from Jules Vern's book, "20.000 Leagues Under the Sea", the Akkorokamui has the reputation of attacking and swamping fishing boats. Many local fishermen carry sickles or large knives to protect them from the monstrous creature.

There are written accounts of the creature throughout the history of the local peoples of Ainu. The Ainu and Their Folklore written by John Batchelor in the early 1900s describe an attack against three fishermen out fishing for swordfish. The great sea monster had large staring eyes, and was round in shape. During the desperate fight the fishermen said the monster emitted a dark fluid and noxious odor. The three men survived the attack, but suffered many days after from the foul smell. They lay trembling in their beds unable to sleep or eat. Other recorded accounts record the size of the creature as being at least 80 meters in length with thick large tentacles the size of a man's torso. In most cases, the creature is described with large eyes.

Could the Akkorokamui exist? In Greek legend and lore there is mention of a great beast known as the kraken which was called by the Gods to do their bidding. The kraken would attack the ships on the seas and sink them. The kraken is also known in the legendary tales of sea monsters off the coast of Norway and Greenland. These tales are probably based on sightings of giant squids that live in the deeper depths of the ocean to rise to the surface to attack ships. In modern times, giant squid hunters have found that many of the squids have the ability to change colors which may also include a brilliant red. It certainly sounds possible the great kraken like giant squids could actually exist, and they may be much larger than we ever anticipated.

INFORMATION SOURCES:

http://en.wikipedia.org/wiki/Akkorokamui

http://www.cryptomundo.com/cryptozoo-news/akkorokamui/

http://www.paranormalknowledge.com/articles/akkorokamui.html

Swancer, Brent via Coleman, Loren. Akkorokamui. Cryptomundo. http://www.cryptomundo.com/cryptozoo-news/akkorokamui

Batchelor, John (1901). *The Ainu and Their Folklore*. London: The Religious Tract Society.

Tierney, Emiko (1984). *Illness and Culture in Japan: an Anthropological View*. Cambridge, Cambridgeshire, New York: Cambridge University Press.

Katao, Miki. Shingyoku & Teramachi-dori: Crossroads of Today and the Past. Learning About Kyoto. Kyoto University of Foreign Studies.http://www.kyopro.kufs.ac.jp/dp/dp01.nsf/b7eb328e75d9627.

ALLIGATOR GIANTS IN ARIZONA

This story has all the makings of an urban legend. Just like the urban legend of Giant Alligators in New York's sewers, Arizona might have monster alligators lurking in their lakes and rivers.

Jack Adams Alligator Farm was a popular tourist attraction during 1950 into 1960. It was located on Main Street in Mesa, next to Hi Jolly. The alligator farm boasted tons of alligators on display.

As a youth, I visited the farm with my parents. I remember the huge sign with a big green Alligator on it. As we paid the admission we entered the area where the outdoor pens were located, and yes there were tons of alligators. There were other reptiles too. Turtles and various types of snakes abound.

One of the activities I remember most was the feeding of the Alligators. My father put me on his shoulders so I could get a bird's eye view of the dead chickens being tossed into the pens. Whenever a chicken would hit the ground, a feeding frenzy would start with the alligators snapping on the chicken and rolling to keep the other alligators away. It amazed me that none of the alligators came away with a missing body part.

Jack Adams Alligator Farm eventually went out of business in the 1960s. The doors and gates were closed to the public. Most of the animals were moved out to other zoos and animal sanctuaries. However, there was a rumor which talked of abandoned alligators left to starve to death.

Several seniors from Mesa High School decided to take action. They made a raid on the alligator farm and removed approximately sixty small alligators. Thinking they were doing the right thing, they released the alligators in the canals, rivers and Saguaro Lake. Of course they had not thought their actions all the way through. Little alligators turn into big alligators under the right conditions. It is actually unknown as to the life span of an alligator. There are some old timers in zoos that are over 76 years old. Some of these giant lizards get 13 to 15 feet in length and weigh over 1000 pounds. (Remember the alligator raid happened only forty years ago).

It didn't take long for the authorities to find start receiving reports of alligators showing up in the irrigation waters, ditches, and on the lawns of the residents of Mesa. There was an immediate round up of the critters. And the officials believed they had captured all of the released critters.

But what if they were wrong?

INFORMATION SOURCES:

http://en.wikipedia.org/wiki/Alligator

http://www.eastvalleytribune.com/article_0da8b48a-3436-5174-952b-4f467ed81be3.html

http://www.phoenixmag.com/lifestyle/history/201106/reptile-dysfunction/

THE ALMAS

The Almas also known as Abnauayu, Almasty, Albasty, Bekk-bok, Biabin-guli, Golub-yayan, Gul-biavan, Auli-avan, Kaptar, Kra-dhun, Ksy-gyik, Ochokochi, Mirygdy, Mulen, Voita, and Wind-man. The term Almas is Mongolian for "Wild man". These creatures are unconfirmed, but there is quite a bit of evidence of their existence. The territory of the Almas includes the Altai Mountains of Southern Mongolia, The Pamir Mountains of Asia, and the Caucasus of Central Asia.

The Almas are reported to be a bipedal primate or hominids which are very human-like. Adults average five to six feet tall, and some reports have them near seven feet, and 300 pounds. They have early human like facial features with a heavy brow line, prominent chin, and flat broad nose. Their bodies are covered with brown hair with a reddish tint. This description brings to mind the image of the caveman.

A sighting was described by Myra Shackley in her article "Still Living?". She reports a 1963 event by pediatrician Ivan Ivlov who was working with Mongolian children. He discovered that many of the children had seen the Almases. Neither was afraid of each other.

Some Crypto zoologists believe the Almas may be related to the Neanderthal, which may lend credence to the story of Zana the wild woman who was thought  to be an Almas who lived among humans in T'khina in the Caucasus near Abkhazia. She was captured in 1850 and soon became part of the village. She gave birth to several children, from a human father. Surviving children grew up to be normal and functional members of the village. Zana died in 1890.

A second captured Almas happened in 1941 by the Red Army. Unfortunately, the male was interrogated by the army, and was either unable or refused to answer questions. He was executed for being a spy. He was reported to be very human like with dark brown hair covering his body.

In recent DNA testing of the Human Race, it was determined that most modern Caucasian Humans have some genes from the Neanderthal. The report goes on to say the genes are not existent in those who originating in Africa. This report seems to indicate that those from Europe must have had children with the Neanderthal in the early beginnings of modern man. This leads to all kinds of speculation.

Could Bigfoot be related to the Almas? Could the Almas be Neanderthal? Could Bigfoot be our cousins?

INFORMATION SOURCES:

http://en.wikipedia.org/wiki/Almas_(cryptozoology)

http://www.unknown-creatures.com/almas.html

http://cryptozoo.monstrous.com/zana.htm

Sjögren, Bengt, *Berömda vidunder*, Settern, 1980, ISBN 91-7586-023-6 **(Swedish)**

Michael Heaney, "Who were the Arismaspeans", web version
with minor additions reproduced from Folklore, volume 104
(1993), pp. 53–66

Newton, Michael (2005). "Almas/Almasti". Encyclopedia of
Cryptozoology: A Global Guide. McFarland & Company, Inc.
p. 19.ISBN 0-7864-2036-7.

Myra Shackley, Antiquity, 56, 31 (1982)

Loren Coleman and Patrick Huyghe (1999). The Field Guide to
Bigfoot and Other Mystery Primates. New York:
HarperCollins.ISBN 1-933665-12-2

A Skeleton Still Buried and a Skull Unearthed: the Story of
Zana (retrieved 23 December 2010]

The Pamirs and the Caucasus region(retrieved 23 December
2010)

Dan Vergano (28 June 2010). "Ancient legends once walked
among early humans?". USA Today. Retrieved 23 January 2011

THE ALTAMAHA-HA

The Altamaha-ha is the "sea serpent" of Georgia. It has been reported in the small streams near the Altamah River of Georgia near the town of Darien. There has been no physical evidence collected of the actual existence, but there have been many accounts of swimmers bumping into the creature. The creature seems to be docile for there have not been any reports of attacks or aggressiveness.

The cryptid has many Loc Ness monster characteristics such as swimming like a dolphin or porpoise undulating through the water with sometimes as many as three humps visible above the water. It is reported to be much like a serpent with a crocodile type snout and fins on the tail. The fins at the end of the tail are oriented horizontally like a dolphin. There are flipper-type fins located where the front shoulders would be located (much like the fins of a seal). The color varies from the top being grey to the whitish-yellow underbelly.

Sightings date from modern to 18th century. The early reports come from the local Talma Indian Tribe inhabiting the area prior to Georgia being settled by the English. The early Indian accounts describe a giant serpent-like creature. Many Crypto zoologists believe the creature may be a sea creature who is returning to the Altamah River for spawning leaving the waters around Darien vacant of the creature for most of the year. Modern sightings have the creature at approximately fifty feet in length, and sometimes include reports of juvenile creatures.

The Altamaha-ha is also known as the Altie who received its nickname from timber workers that spotted the creature swimming in the shallow waters near the river in 1920. Another report came from the Boy Scouts in 1940 and was backed up by a report from two Reidsville State Prison officials in 1950. In 2002, a man pulling a boat up the river near Brunswick spotted the cryptid which was over twenty feet in length and was approximately six feet wide at the widest part. It seemed to have surfaced for air and then submerged back into the river.

Other sea monsters of this nature are the Ogopogo (Okanagan Lake, in British Columbia, Canada), Skin Fin (Lake Powell, of Arizona), and Champ (states of Vermont and New York) but partially situated across the Canada-United States border in the Canadian province of Quebec).

INFORMATION SOURCES:

A video of the Altamaha-ha may be seen at http://www.youtube.com/watch?v=kqy0lGizXV4

http://en.wikipedia.org/wiki/Altamaha-ha

http://cryptidz.wikia.com/wiki/Altamaha-ha

http://www.visitdarien.com/altamaha-ha.html

http://georgiamysteries.blogspot.com/2008/05/legend-of-altamaha-ha.html

http://www.cryptomundo.com/cryptotourism/georgias-altamaha-ha/

Vivlamore, Barbara (August 29, 2006). "CLOSER LOOK AT ... State's 'Altie' tale". *The Atlanta Journal-Constitution* (in English). pp. 4E.

Crenshaw, Holly (February 26, 2001). "eMETRO". *The Atlanta Journal and Constitution* (in English). pp. 2B.

Ferguson, Anna (May 13, 2009). "McIntosh showcases a new mascot". *The Brunswick News* (in English) (Georgia).

THE AMERANTHROPOIDES LOSI (DE LOY'S APE)

(FAIR USE DOCTRINE FOR EDUCATIONAL PURPOSES ONLY)

The Ameranthropoides loysi (De Loy's Ape) is reported to be a large primate living in the jungles between Columbia and Venezuela. There is only one photo of the creature, and it looks very much like a Spider Monkey. The photo was taken by an expedition led by François De Loysin 1920. De Loys was a Swiss geologist looking for oil in the Tarra

Riverarea. The expedition entered the jungle with twenty men and returned with only four survivors. They found no oil, and the running battles with the natives coupled with diseases of the jungles took a heavy toll.

The cryptid was killed by the expedition members. They reported two creatures, one male and one female. These cryptids were very agitated as the approached the expedition members while making wild waving gestures, screaming and throwing feces at the humans. The female ran away when the male was shot and killed. Deloys measured the body as being 1.57 meters (5.2 feet) tall. This was larger than the normal Spider Monkey. Another interesting item was the number of teeth. The specimen had thirty two teeth where most monkeys have thirty six teeth. There was no tail. It might be noted Spider Monkeys are not found in the area Deloys' expedition was traveling.

Deloys had the body propped up on a box with a stick holding up the head to pose the body for the photograph. Afterwards, the body was skinned. They kept the head and hide, and disposed of the body. Unfortunately, the head and hide was lost during the struggles of the expedition.

Many believe De Loys' Ape to be a hoax. The general consensus from the skeptics is the photo is that of a Spider Monkey made to look larger through perspective photography. One of the skeptics was Sir Arthur Keith, a well known anthropologist, stating there was only one photo, and it does not show the lack of a tail.

Loren Coleman, a modern crypto zoologist, also believes the photo is a hoax by pointing out the cryptid is actually smaller than De Loys' claim and states the deception may have been proposed by De Loys' friend George Montandon (an anthropologist). It was Montandon who suggested the name "Ameranthropoides loysi" proposing the cryptid was the ancestor of the "Red "people of the Western Hemisphere and possibly the Missing Link.

Some Crypto zoologists remain steadfast denying the hoax. Would De Loys take the time, effort, and resources to perpetrate such a hoax when his expedition was in such dire straits? They lost sixteen men, the head and hide, and taking photos was not such an easy task in the 1920s.

INFORMATION SOURCES:

http://www.youtube.com/watch?v=Aax7vJ32whc

http://en.wikipedia.org/wiki/Ameranthropoides_loysi

http://www.weird-encyclopedia.com/de-Loys-ape.php

http://blogs.scientificamerican.com/history-of-geology/2012/10/07/de-loys-ape/

Jerome Clark, Unexplained! 347 Strange Sightings, Incredible Occurrences, and Puzzling Physical Phenomena (Visible Ink Press, 1993).

Bernard Heuvelmans, On The Track Of Unknown Animals (Hill and Wang, 1958).

Michael Shoemaker, "The Mystery of Mono Grande", Strange Magazine, April 1991.

Karl P.N. Shuker, Extraordinary Animals Revisited (CFZ Press, 2007).

Bernardo Urbani and Angel L. Viloria, Ameranthropoides loysi Montandon 1929: the History of a Primatological Fraud / Ameranthropoides Loysi Montandon 1929: la historia de un fraude primatologico (Libros en Red, 2009).

THE AMOMONGO

The Amomongo (Negros Ape) is an unconfirmed
primate said to exist on the Negros Island of the
Philippines . The local people believe the cryptid
lives in caves at the base of Mt. Kanlaon and they
sometimes call the creature the "wild monkey". It is
described as being gorilla-like and stands about five
and one half feet tall. It is hairy and the hands
support long nails or claws. The nails are used as
weapons to disembowel its prey such as chickens,
goats and other small animals. The hair is white and

the creature is generally reclusive staying away from humans.

Even though there are officially no great apes in the Philippines (other than zoos), there have been many sightings of the Amomongo. On 9 June and following day and night of 10 June, 2008; an event was reported to the police and Mayor Alberto Nicor by two residents Elias Galves and Salvador Aguilar. The two men were attacked, but managed to escape suffering several wounds. Animals in the area were gutted and the creature was devouring the entrails.

The Police launched an investigation and were able to confirm the attacks on the men and animals through various other local witnesses. Mayor Nicor believes the Amomongo is a wild animal and not a witch or Aswang. He believes the cryptid was driven from the hills by hunger or human encroachment, and it was desperate enough to venture into the human's village. However, the villagers were quick to arm themselves with arrows and weapons to protect themselves and their live stock.

Many crypto zoologists believe this cryptid is a hoax. They point out apes are not white, but this does not account for the possibility of an albino. The skeptics also point out there are no great apes in the Philippines. However, they do not account for the dense jungles of the Philippines. In 1971,

anthropologists discovered an unknown tribe of
native humans the Tasaday.

Those who believe the account of the attacks say it
would be very difficult to pull off such a hoax. The
sheer number of animals slaughtered, the locations,
and number of credible witnesses would be very hard
for any one person to accomplish. The Pilipino police
are a no non-sense group. They have a reputation of
shooting and then sorting things out later. A hoaxer
or team of hoaxers would not only have to survive the
police, but they would have to face the farmers who
would certainly solve the problem. The risk of being
caught is not worth the hoax.

INFORMATION SOURCES:

http://en.wikipedia.org/wiki/Amomongo

http://www.cryptomundo.com/cryptozoo-news/amomongo/

http://www.sunstar.com.ph/bacolod/lifestyle/2011/08/20/mystery-amomongo-174214

http://www.unexplained-mysteries.com/forum/index.php?showtopic=218477

Bayoran, Gilbert (2008-06-13). "Creature terrorizing residents of farms". Visayan Daily Star. Retrieved 2008-06-20.

Delilan, Erwin Ambo (2008-06-16). "Residents on alert vs 'wild monkey'". Sun.Star Bacolod. Retrieved 2008-06-20.

THE ANDEAN WOLF

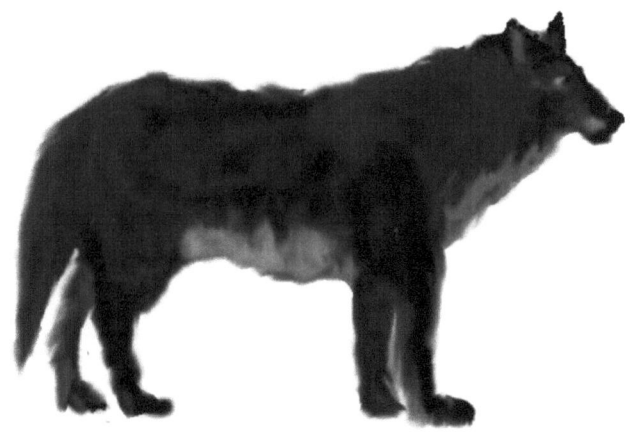

The Andean Wolf has been shrouded in mystery as to
its actual existence. This is one of the
few cryptids that were discovered not by sightings or
legends, but by its pelt. An animal dealer in Buenos
Airessold three pelts to Lorenz Hagenbeck in 1927.
The pelts were professed by the dealer to be from a
wild dog in the Andes. The pelts eventually ended up
in Germany where it was inspected by Dr. Ingo
Krumbiegel. The Doctor determined the pelts to be
from an unknown/un-described species in 1940. Dr.
Kumbiegel had found a skull in the Andes
approximately 10 years before examining the pelt,
and he believed the pelt and skull were from the same
type of creature. He pointed out the differences in
the Maned wolf (24 cm in length) which had a much
smaller skull than the Andean Wolf (31 cm). The

Doctor presented a paper and suggested it's scientific name of Dasycycon hagenbecki. Unfortunately, 1945 was not a good time due to World War II. The paper was lost and was never peer reviewed. In the world of science, this means no proof. Science will not accept the discovery of anything unless it has been under a thorough peer review.

Eventually science developed DNA testing, and the pelts were tested in the 1960s. The Scientists proclaimed the pelt to belong to a domestic dog. The pelt was retested by the Munich Zoological Museum in the year 2000. They found the test to be inconclusive due to the pelt being chemically treated and contaminated with pig, wolf, and human DNA.

The Andean Wolf has also been known as the Hagenback Wolf, Andean Mountain Wolf, and received the scientific name of Dasycyon hagenbecki. They are believed to be indigenous to the High Andes of South America.

There is a possibility of mistaken identity. In 1782, the Patagonian Red Fox and Fuegian Fox were recorded and described scientifically and puts them ranging throughout the Andes. Another creature known as Culpeo, Pseudalopex culpaeus has also been referred or believed to be the Andean Wolf by some crypto-zoologists. There are other references made to discovery of the Andean wolf in 1910 and 1949. However, the Andean Wolf is still considered to be unproven.

INFORMATION SOURCES:

http://en.wikipedia.org/wiki/Andean_wolf

http://cryptozoology.wikia.com/wiki/Andean_Wolf

https://www.google.com/search?q=andean+wolf&tbm=isch&tbo=u&source=univ&sa=X&ei=xR9wUqf8BaSDjAKV9IDAAQ&sqi=2&ved=0CDIQsAQ&biw=1008&bih=526

Heuvelmans, Bernard. "*On the Track of Unknown Animals*". Farrar Straus & Giroux, January 1965. ISBN 0-8090-7451-6.

Shuker, Karl. "*The New Zoo: New and Rediscovered Animals of the Twentieth Century*". House of Stratus, 2002. ISBN 1-84232-561-2

A review of canid classification. American Museum novitates ; no. 2646

Eberhart, George M. *Mysterious Creatures: A Guide to Cryptozoology*. 2 vols. Santa Barbara, California: ABC-CLIO, 2002.

THE ASWANG

During my stay in the Philippines, I got to know many of the residents and they shared many of their stories of cryptid creatures within the country. Probably the most feared was the Aswang. This name is a multi meaning term for all types of shape-shifters, witches, vampires, werewolves, and manananggals. My Filipino friends describe the Aswang as being a vampire-like creatures that eats the dead.

Some of the local names are "tik-tik", "wak-wak", "soc-soc" and "Aso ang". The myths and legends of the Aswang are well known throughout the Philippines dating as far back as the 16th century. An interesting aspect of the Awang is they are usually depicted as being female.

It is very hard to describe a shape shifter, and of course there are no photos of any such type of creature. During the day an Aswang can show themselves as a village resident, but at night they can transform into pigs, dogs, birds, cats, or other known creatures. They are silent and fast and can be as thin as a bed post. Some make noises like the clicking of a clock thus the name "Tik-Tik". One method of spotting a Aswang is by the blood shot eyes which are caused by staying up all night searching for houses where bodies are laid for their wake the next morning. They intend to steal the bodies. Usually, the bodies are collected and deposited in a nest at the base of a large tree where the Aswang can hide the evidence by covering it up with leaves, and plant material.

When the Aswang appears human, it is usually the appearance of an old hag (witchy appearance). She will sometimes make a duplicate of her intended victim from a banana stock and it comes alive and goes to the home of the victim and soon becomes sick and dies. The Aswang kidnaps the victim and take them back to her lair to eat them. They are reported to prefer eating the liver first.

Almost any bizarre incident, such as kidnapped children, miscarriages, strange noises, grave robberies, and eccentric people with peculiar habits are blamed on the Aswang. It is believed by most these myths are meant to frighten children to keep them off the streets and in their homes at night. Some of the defenses against the Awang are adorning homes with garlic bulbs, holy water and other objects believed to repel Aswang.

To kill an Aswang several methods are available. Spraying it with hot sauce, or garlic will do the trick. If you have a bladed weapon, you can behead it, or if you can set it on fire. Burning it will kill it.

INFORMATION SOURCES:

http://en.wikipedia.org/wiki/Aswang

http://www.pantheon.org/articles/a/aswang.html

http://thefilmpolice.blogspot.com/2012/10/feature-top-5-ways-to-kill-aswang.html

Scott, William Henry (1994). *Barangay: Sixteenth Century Philippine Culture and Society*. Quezon City: Ateneo de Manila University Press. ISBN 971-550-135-4.

Tan, Michael (2008-10-26). "Aswang! Aswang!". *Sunday Inquirer Magazine*

Cruz, Neal (2008-10-31). "As I See It: Philippine mythological monsters". *Philippine Daily Inquirer*

Eugenio, Damiana (2002). *Philippine Folk Literature: The Legends*. Matt Asombrado Paculba City: University of the Philippines Press. p. 490. ISBN 971-542-357-4.

Ramos, Maximo D. (1971). *Creatures of Philippine Lower Mythology*. Quezon City: University of the Philippines Press. ISBN 971-06-0691-3.

Ocampo, Ambeth (2010-02-16). "Looking Back: 'Aswang' and counter-insurgency". *Philippine Daily Inquirer*

THE AYIA NAPA SEA MONSTER

Sea Monster cryptids are always interesting because we do not know what lurks in the depths of the sea. Just about the time science thinks they know it all, a new creature is reported or found. There is always the possibility of fantastic beasts swimming the sea to emerge from time to time to astound maritime travelers. I have fished the oceans of the world, and I can attest to catching some sea creatures I have not been able to identify. You never know what will be at the other end of your line.

The Ayia Napa Sea Monster is a bit different from the other reported sea serpents. It is referred to by the local fishermen as the "To Filiko Teras" (The

Friendly Monster). It has never been reported to be harmful or attacking the boats to sink the ships or eat the passengers. Although it has been reported to rip holes in the fishing nets or drag the nets away.

The cryptid is generally found along the coast of Ayia Napa of Cyprus in the Mediterranean sea in the area of area known as Kokkinochoria island. Some descriptions report it to be a crocodile or serpent like creature with a woman's torso and serpent like body. Reports ancient Greeks add more intrigue by adding six snarling dog heads protruding from the midriff, each supported by two forelimbs.

The sea monster has become quite famous in the region and is a well known tourist attraction. It has been dubbed the "Cyprus Loch Ness" monster. The countless sightings and reports of the Creature from the Depths have appeared in t he local newspapers, and many claim it to be the mythical sea monster of Greek mythology called Scylla. The likeness of the creature is a popular design used in pottery, vases, bowls and paintings from both modern and ancient artists.

The creature eventually caught the attention of the local government. The Ministry of Fisheries and Marine Affairs has determined the countless reports warrant further investigation. They have decided to attempt to capture the sea monster. The bait to lure the creature from the depths of the waters will be live chickens and raw meat. Authorities hope the capture of such a creature will be a boom to the tourist industry, and will build a facility to display the creature if and when it is caught.

INFORMATION SOURCES:

http://en.wikipedia.org/wiki/Ayia_Napa_sea_monster

http://cryptozoo-oscity.blogspot.com/2009/08/ayia-napa-sea-monster-investigations.html

HadjiPavlou, P (March 14, 2007). "To Filiko Teras". Cyprus Weekly. p. 18.

Alethea Reynolds (28 October 2008). "Cyprus officials search for mystery 'monster'". Famagusta Gazette. Retrieved 2009-12-29.

Department of Antiquities, Republic Of Cyprus

ABOUT THE AUTHOR

Mitchell's relatives were some of the first Pioneers to settle Arizona. Mitch was born in St Johns and grew up in Mesa. After graduating from Mesa High School, Mitch joined the Air Force as an Airman Basic, and worked his way through the ranks to Major. He became one of the five Space Operations Officers in the military that advised the General in NORAD/USSPACECOMMAND on space technologies and capabilities. Nothing got into or out of the world's atmosphere without him knowing

about it. Mitch retired from the Military in 1993 and
worked for several aerospace and semiconductor
companies until the present.

Mitchell started studying Cryptozoology in 2008, and
became Arizona's number 1 Bigfoot researcher.
During this time he has successfully photographed
and videoed the Mogollon Monster (Arizona's
Bigfoot) numerous times. He has amassed a large
collection of supporting evidence, such as footprints,
handprints, hair, eye witness accounts, and
vocalizations. All of this may be viewed at
MogollonMonster.com on the internet. Mitch's
research on the Bigfoot has become very popular with
over 1,800, 000 views on You-tube videos under the
user name SusanFarns.

Mitch is also a prolific writer and has many books
and DVDs published by Southwest Publications and
are available through Amazon.com and any local
bookstore. The listing of books and DVDs are:

ALL OF THESE PRODUCTS ARE AVAILABLE THROUGH AMAZON.COM, CREATESPACE.COM, BARNS AND NOBLE, BOOKSTORES, AND BOOK DISTIRBUTORS.

Bigfoot in Arizona, Documentary, Part 1

Synopsis: On Memorial Day, 2008; MogollonMonster.com was formed to investigate Bigfoot sightings in Arizona. This Documentary video contains real research findings and may appear to be rough and fast is some spots. In some cases, you can tell the researchers are very nervous about the surroundings they have entered, Price: $11.95
Directed by Mitch Waite Runtime: 58 minutes Release year: 2011
Studio: MogollonMonster.com Productions ASIN: B005BCRE2O (Rental) and B005BCRDRK (Purchase)

Bigfoot In Arizona, Documentary, Part 2 Close Encounters , Mitchell Waite

(Director), MogollonMonster.com (Studio) , List Price: $11.95, 60 minutes, NTSC, UPC: 886470301782 , The MogollonMonster.com Team takes on a major expedition to learn more about Arizona's Bigfoot. During a night ops event, they run into something that is not happy at them. Later in the night, something comes to their camp.

Bigfoot Shelters And Nests , Mitch Waite (Director), Mogollon Monster

Studios (Studio) , List Price: $11.95, 93 minutes, NTSC UPC: 886470337798 The MogollonMonster.com team has spent four years compiling data, photos, and video of Bigfoot homes, shelters and hunting blinds. Where do they sleep? What is their social structure like? And Much more.

Bigfoot Research 2009, Major Mitchell Waite (Director),

MogollonMonster.com Productions (Studio), List Price: $11.95
93 minutes, NTSC, UPC: 886470563418, Chronological documentation videos of Bigfoot research of the Mogollon Monster, Arizona's Bigfoot. These videos record the progress, findings, events and encounters of the MogollonMonster.com research team on the Mogollon Rim of Arizona.

42

Chasing the Mogollon Monster, Arizona's Bigfoot (DVD), Mitchell Waite

(Producer), MogollonMonster.com (Studio), The Mogollon Monster Team (Actors) , List Price: $9.95, 56 minutes, NTSC, UPC: 886470006137, A selection of documentary film clips of Bigfoot researchers chasing the Mogollon Monster, Arizona's Bigfoot. Location is on the Mogollon Rim in Arizona. The team locates footprints, nests, scat, and experiences many vocalizations.

The Mogollon Monster, Arizona's Bigfoot, Authored by Susan Farnsworth ,

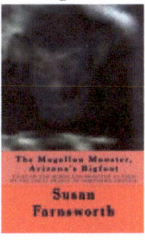

List Price: $9.95 , 5" x 8" (12.7 x 20.32 cm), Black & White on White paper, 110 pages , ISBN-13: 978-1461016267 , ISBN-10: 1461016266
BISAC: Nature / Wildlife, A collection of campfire stories of the Mogollon Monster, Arizona's Bigfoot as told by the Locals of Northern Arizona

More Mogollon Monster, Arizona's Bigfoot, Authored by Susan Farnsworth,

Authored with Maj Mitchell Waite
List Price: $9.95 5" x 8" (12.7 x 20.32 cm), **Black & White** on White paper, 124 pages, ISBN-13: 978-1468064711, ISBN-10: 1468064711 , BISAC: Nature / Wildlife, Part 1: More tales of the Mogollon Monster, Arizona's Bigfoot compiled from the locals of Northern Arizona. Part 2: Actual Bigfoot field research conducted by MogollonMonster.com

Have You Ever Seen A UFO?, Authored by Susan Farnsworth, List Price:

$8.95, 5" x 8" (12.7 x 20.32 cm), Black & White on White paper, 100 pages, ISBN-13: 978-1461102397, ISBN-10: 1461102391
BISAC: Social Science / General, A selection of interviews with those who would know about UFOs--Our Military. Was Roswell real? Are there little green men?

Blood, Gold, And The Superstition Mountains, Authored by Mr. Mitchell
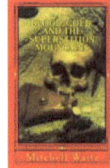
Waite, List Price: $9.95, 5" x 8" (12.7 x 20.32 cm), Black &
White on White paper 196 pages, ISBN-13: 978-1461096153
ISBN-10: 1461096154, BISAC: Fiction / Historical, An
action/adventure thriller based on the legends and lore of the
Lost Dutchman's Gold Mine and the Superstition Mountains of
Arizona. Based on real people, places, events and treasure
maps.

Blood, Gold, And The Superstition Mountains, The Return, Authored by

Mitchell Waite List Price: $9.95 5" x 8" (12.7 x 20.32 cm),
Black & White on White paper 134 pages, ISBN-13: 978-
1461115502 ISBN-10: 1461115507, BISAC: Fiction /
Mystery & Detective / General, An exciting action/thriller
adventure story of the Lost Dutchman Gold Mine as it takes
place in modern times. Based on history, real people, and
events, this fictional novel will keep you glued to your seats till
the end.

The Continuing Search for the Lost Dutchman's Gold Mine, Authored by
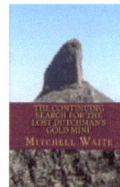
Mitchell Waite List Price: $9.95, 5" x 8" (12.7 x 20.32 cm),
Black & White on White paper, 152 pages, ISBN-13: 978-
1461016229, ISBN-10: 1461016223, BISAC: History /
United States / State & Local / Southwest, A study and
research of the Lost Dutchman's Gold Mine in the
Superstition Mountains of Arizona

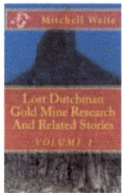
Lost Dutchman Gold Mine Research And Related Stories,
Authored by Maj Mitchell Waite   List Price: $14.95 , 5" x 8"
(12.7 x 20.32 cm)   Black & White on White paper, 196 pages
ISBN-13: 978-1466230385 ISBN-10: 146623038X, BISAC:
History / United States / State & Local / Southwest, A unique
twist on research for the Lost Dutchman's Gold Mine and the
related stories of the Superstition Mountains

Desert Gold   Authored by Major Mitchell Waite, List Price: $9.95 5" x 8"

(12.7 x 20.32 cm)   Black & White on White paper, 156
pages, ISBN-13: 978-1463777067, ISBN-10: 146377706X,
BISAC: Drama / American, A tale of love, lost gold, and
treachery in the Superstition Mountains of Arizona. A true
western novel based on the legends and lore and history of
Arizona.

Gold Panning Equipment, Build Your Own, Authored by Mitchell Waite

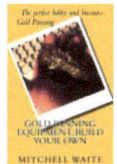

List Price: $8.95   5" x 8" (12.7 x 20.32 cm) Black & White on White paper 80 pages ISBN-13: 978-1461135951, ISBN-10: 1461135958, BISAC: Crafts & Hobbies / General, Instructions and plans to build effective gold extraction equipment.

Backyard Gold Panning, The Perfect Part Time Job, Authored by Maj

Mitchell Waite, List Price: $16.95, 8" x 10" (20.32 x 25.4 cm), Full Color on White paper, 74 pages, ISBN-13: 978-1470053512, ISBN-10: 1470053519, BISAC: Sports & Recreation / Outdoor Skills, Set up to gold pan in your backyard. Easy to do, and its a great part time job. With gold approaching $2000 per Troy Oz, it can be very profitable. This book tells how to pan, where to dig, various pieces of extraction equipment, and maps to go find your gold.

READING TREASURE MAP SIGNS AND SYMBOLS, Authored by

Mitchell Waite Product Description, An in depth study of reading treasure maps symbol by symbol. The book also proposes solutions for several well known Spanish treasure maps and symbols found in the Superstition Mountains of Arizona. It goes even further and discusses cactus markers for treasure trails in the deserts of the Southwest US and Mexico. List price: $19.95 Paperback: 124 pages, (Language: English, ISBN-10: 1463685513, ISBN-13: 978-1463685515

ATVs, Build Your Own From Scratch, Authored by Mitchell Waite,

Designed by Shannon Waite, List Price: $12.95, 8.5" x 11" (21.59 x 27.94 cm), Full Color on White paper, 46 pages ISBN-13: 978-1466485112, ISBN-10: 1466485116 BISAC: Transportation / General, Step by step instructions on how to build and assemble an ATV from scratch. Totally illustrated with diagrams and photographs. This ATV also features roll bars and cage for safety. Designed for a top speed of 45 MPH.

The SKS 7.62X39 mm Rifle Disassembly And Cleaning Guide , Authored by

Maj Mitchell Waite, List Price: $9.95 5.25" x 8" (13.335 x 20.32 cm), Full Color on White paper, 36 pages, ISBN-13: 978-1468119718, ISBN-10: 1468119710 BISAC: Sports & Recreation / Shooting, Complete disassembly and cleaning instructions for the SKS 7.62mm Rifle.

Esperanza Breathe, Authored by Norma Matheson , List Price: $9.95, 5" x 8"
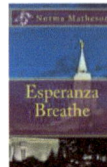 (12.7 x 20.32 cm), Black & White on White paper, 248 pages,
ISBN-13: 978-1468091489, ISBN-10: 1468091484 , BISAC:
Fiction / Christian / Romance
An action packed romance thriller written for Mormons and
other Christian faiths. A story of a young woman's struggle
with her drug biological drug cartel family she has never
known. They learn of her existence and decide to eliminate her
because of her new found FBI friend.

Superstition Mountains Photos And Points of Interest, Authored by Maj
  Mitchell Waite, List Price: $14.95, 8" x 10" (20.32 x 25.4 cm),
Full Color on White paper, 46 pages, ISBN-13: 978-
1475214215, ISBN-10: 1475214219
BISAC: **Nature / Regional,** Full color photos and Topographic
Maps of points of interest in the Superstition Mountains of
Arizona.

The Round Valley Miracle, Authored by Maj Mitchell Waite, List Price: $8.95,
 5" x 8" (12.7 x 20.32 cm), Black & White on White paper, 66
pages, ISBN-13: 978-1466270244, ISBN-10: 1466270241,
BISAC: **Fiction / Religious,** Cowboys and Angels. A story of
the struggle the Pioneer settlers when called to settle the upper
head waters of the Little Colorado River of the territory of
Arizona in a pace called Round Valley.

NEW RELEASES

BIGFOOT RESEARCH 2010, PART 1, MITCHELL WAITE
 (DIRECTOR), MOGOLLONMONSTER.COM,
(STUDIO), LIST PRICE: $12.95, 113 MINUTES, NTSC ,
UPC: 886470605095 , CHRONOLOGICAL VIDEO
DOCUMENTATION OF THE BIGFOOT RESEARCH
BEING CONDUCTED ON THE MOGOLLON RIM OF
ARIZONA. VIDEO TITLES ARE:
ANOTHER LOOK AT BIGFOOT
BIGFOOT ROAD BLOCKS
BIGFOOT GAME CAMERA RESULTS
MOGOLLON MONSTER HUNTING
NOT A BIGFOOT
BIGFOOT FACE ANALYSIS
BIGFOOT NESTS AND GUARD STATIONS
BIGFOOT NESTS THE RETURN

BIGFOOT HUNTING TECHNIQUES

Bigfoot Research 2010, Part 2

Mitchell Waite (Director), MogollonMonster.com Studio (Studio) List Price: $12.95, 113 minutes, NTSC, UPC: 886470608157, This DVD documentary records the events, findings, and theories of the MogollonMonster.com research team for the year 2010. THE VIDEOS CONTAINED IN THIS DVD ARE: BIGFOOR CAMPFIRE DISCUSSION (8 VIDEOS) FIRST SIGHTING IN JUNE (2 VIDEOS) BIGFOOT NEST? VERY INTRIGUING FOOTAGE BIGFOOT NESTS, OLD ROOT CELLAR BIGFOOT BED OR GRAVE

BIGFOOT RESEARCH 2010 PART 3, MITCH WAITE (DIRECTOR),

MOGOLLONMONSTER.COM SUDIO (STUDIO) , LIST PRICE: **$12.95, 113 MINUTES,** NTSC, UPC, 886470610082, REAL BIGFOOT RESEARCH CONDUCTED ON THE MOGOLLON RIM OF ARIZONA. THIS DVD COMPILES THE EVENTS, FINDINGS, AND THEORIES OF THE MOGOLLONMONSTER.COM RESEARCH TEAM. VIDEOS WITH IN THE DVD ARE: BIGFOOT NEST VERY INTRIGUING FOOTAGE, BIGFOOT HUNTING TECHNIQUES, MYSTERIOUS DIRT DRAWINGS, BIGFOOT EQUIPMENT CHECKOUT, BIGFOOT GARDEN OF EDEN PROJECT, SCOUTING NEW BIGFOOT AREA, BIGFOOT OR BEAR, BIGFOOT ROAD HUNTING, BIGFOOT SIGHTING, ANOTHER LOOK AT BIGFOOT , BIGFOOT RESEARCH, WHAT IS IT, BIGFOOT SNOW TRACKING, BIGFOOT HEAD ANALYSIS BIGFOOT RESEARCH CAMERA RETRIEVAL

BIGFOOT RESEARCH 2010, PART 4 (DVD)

Mitchell Waite (Director), MogollonMonster.com (Studio), The Mogollon Monster Team Members (Actors), List Price: **$10.95, 20 minutes,** NTSC, UPC: 886470900954, 2011 season wrap up. The team obtains a not human fingerprint and collects some very interesting game camera footage. , Bigfoot Fingerprints' , First Bigfoot Outing 2010 , analysis of Bigfoot Footage , Bushnell Game Camera Results , Searching For Bigfoot , Bigfoot, Wolves, and Coyotes, OH MY , Bigfoot Mischief , Bigfoot Research

BIGFOOT RESEARCH 2011, PART 1 (DVD), MITCHELL WAITE (DIRECTOR), MOGOLLONMONSTER.COM (STUDIO), MOGOLLONMONSTER.COM TEAM MEMBERS (ACTORS), LIST PRICE: **$11.95**

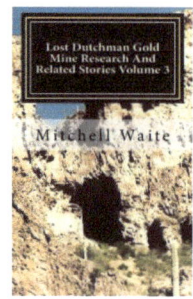

126 minutes, NTSC, UPC: 887936132018, Bigfoot Research 5 Jan 2011, Monitoring Bigfoot's Territory 18 Jan 2011, Bigfoot In Our Camp, Bigfoot Perspective, Drive through Bigfoot Hot Zone, Bigfoot Research 4 Feb 2011, Bigfoot Research 22 Feb 2011, Bigfoot Smell, and Bigfoot Smell a Week Later, Bigfoot Research 8 March 2011

BIGFOOT RESEARCH 2011 PART 2 (DVD) MogollonMonster.com

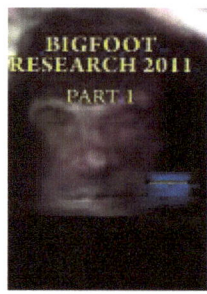

(Studio), Mitch Waite, Susan Farnsworth, David Waite, and Alex Hearn (Actors), List Price: **$11.95, 123 minutes,** NTSC, UPC: 887936515705, Fourteen videos make up this DVD. The footage was taken by Bigfoot Researchers while working the Mogollon Rim of Arizona. This is actual documentation video, and not the hyped-up TV program. The reasearch is real. Share the success and failures of the researchers. This video has the Bigfoot Research series, Bigfoot Surveilance Footage, Bigfoot Expedition Footage, Giant Bigfoot Stick Structure Investigation, Sightings from Susan Farnsworth, and Game Camera Footage of An Unknown Animal attacking the camera.

Lost Dutchman Gold Mine Research And Related Stories Volume 3: Black

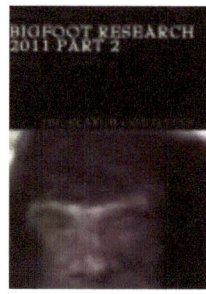

and White Edition, Authored by Maj Mitchell Waite, List Price: **$11.95, 5" x 8"** (12.7 x 20.32 cm) , Black & White on White paper, 156 pages, ISBN-13: 978-1490520667, ISBN-10: 149052066X BISAC: History / Expeditions & Discoveries, This black and white book edition contains newsletters designed to keep expedition team members informed of research, findings, and expedition events in their search for the Lost Dutchman's Gold Mine of Arizona--The Mother of all lost mines and treasures.

Solar Photovoltaic System Economic Analysis for the Electric Energy

Consumer, Authored by Dan Catlin, Literary editor Mitchell Waite, List Price: **$12.95**, **6" x 9"** (15.24 x 22.86 cm) , Full Color on White paper
40 pages, ISBN-13: 978-1483995441, ISBN-10: 1483995445, BISAC: Technology & Engineering / General, This book addresses the issues and benefits of converting to Solar Power. Is solar right for your power consumption needs? What are the costs? Are there incentives to go Solar? Learn more about both commercial and private solar packages.

NOTES:

www.ingramcontent.com/pod-product-compliance
Lightning Source LLC
Chambersburg PA
CBHW050823290526
45792CB00001B/230